CHAKRA JOURNAL

CHAKRA JOURNAL

CREATIVE PROMPTS AND PRACTICES TO OPEN AND ALIGN YOUR CHAKRAS

ALIA SOBEL

ROCKRIDGE
PRESS

Copyright © 2022 by Rockridge Press

All rights reserved. No part of this publication may be reproduced, stored in a retrieval system, or transmitted in any form or by any means, electronic, mechanical, photocopying, recording, scanning, or otherwise without the prior written permission of the Publisher. Requests to the Publisher for permission should be addressed to the Permissions Department, Rockridge Press, 1955 Broadway, Suite 400, Oakland, CA 94612.

First Rockridge Press trade paperback edition 2022

Rockridge Press and the Rockridge Press logo are trademarks or registered trademarks of Callisto Media Inc. and/or its affiliates in the United States and other countries and may not be used without written permission.

For general information on our other products and services, please contact our Customer Care Department within the United States at (866) 744-2665, or outside the United States at (510) 253-0500.

Paperback ISBN: 979-8-88608-090-2

Manufactured in the United States of America

Interior and Cover Designer: Karmen Lizzul
Art Producer: Melissa Malinowsky
Editor: Kahlil Thomas
Production Manager: Lanore Coloprisco

Illustrations © Shutterstock, cover and pp ii, x, 2, 5, 20, 22, 25, 36, 34, 39, 48, 50, 53, 68, 70, 73, 90, 92, 95, 108, 110, 113, 128; Cecilia Morales/Noun Project, p.19; Author photo courtesy of Nichole MCH Photography; All other illustrations used under license from Rainbow Designs/Noun Project

10 9 8 7 6 5 4 3 2 1 0

This book belongs to

_____

INTRODUCTION

Hi, I'm Alia, and I'm so glad you're here!

Do you ever find yourself asking why you're here on Earth? Why any of us are? Understanding these thoughts, and our purpose here, is an ever-evolving journey. Understanding energy is the best place to begin.

I'm yoga certified and a certified Holy Fire and Usui Reiki master teacher, best-selling author, and kick-ass energy coach. All the spiritual energy work I have done has revealed my soul purpose as a light worker, energy healer, and psychic channeler helping the collective heal, awaken, and glow.

This life force energy—aka *you*—and your well-being are directly related to your chakra health. I hope that this informative, interactive journal serves as a personal energy guide, helping you connect to your energy chakras and your inner wisdom, learn more about yourself, and step into self-healing, balancing, and unblocking chakras. This deep self-love helps keep your energy magical, sparkly, and fresh.

I use the phrase "Energy is everything" a lot. Pause for a moment and think about everything happening around you and within you. Do you feel like their energies are linked?

My own life experiences of forty years have taught me about the importance of taking care of my soul, internal energy, and chakras. Like many of you, I have moved through major life moments that I call *energy shifts*: from educating myself through college, living on my own, getting married, having children, moving out of state, and then reaching a traumatic time in my life when I felt numb and lost. Having deep layers of postpartum depression and anxiety paved the way to my understanding of energy and soul work. My own struggle revealed my greatest strengths, teachings, and triumphs.

It's powerful to stop and think about all the things in your life that shift your energy, elevate your soul, and challenge and enlighten you.

I write this journal from my soul to yours, to help you become more deeply connected to your wisdom and the internal energy of your chakras. You were born into this world as the energy of light and love, and you should feel that throughout all the life stages, ups and downs—the exciting, the mundane, and the in-between—of your life. Throughout it all you should stay connected to the most important thing in this entire world: you, your inner light and love, your soul, and your energy.

HOW TO USE THIS BOOK

Chakra is the Sanskrit word for "wheel." You can think of chakras as wheels of free-flowing, positive energy. We have seven major chakras along our spinal column, each associated with sounds, colors, affirmations, and foods. You've probably heard people talk about unblocking their chakras, referring to the idea that when all our chakras are healthy and open, healthy energy can run through them freely and harmony exists among the physical body, mind, and soul. Harmony, peace, and balance sure do sound amazing, right?

Chakras can indeed become closed or stagnant, causing you to feel low-vibe, depressed, anxious, or stressed. I want you to feel open, in a flow state, and filled with love, compassion, and purpose.

All chakras flow with different purpose and intention, and working through them is best done sequentially. We begin at the root (the base of the spine), where we learn to feel safe and secure while being authentic. Next, we flow upward to the sacral chakra, the home of the emotional body, where we discover how to feel our emotions without being overly driven by them. Above this is the solar plexus, the epicenter of the mental body and confidence, where we must confront limiting opinions, judgments, and beliefs so we can cultivate true self-acceptance and willpower.

Next, the heart chakra is the bridge between the lower and upper chakras. Once we have generated the deep self-love required to keep the heart open, we are ready to move into the higher frequencies of the upper chakras. The throat chakra is a most important hub for freedom, release, expressing truths, and manifesting, or turning thoughts into reality. We then move to the third eye chakra—the center of strong intuition and clarity, which finally leads to the crown chakra, which opens us to a boundless sense of trust, oneness, and connection.

The teachings, practices, and activities in this journal will take you through this pathway of connecting to all seven chakras, keeping them healthy, clear, and open.

I hope that by diving in you will gain a deeper appreciation and awareness of the internal energy you send to your chakras, strengthening your light and magic. Energy-filling actions help you become your own guru. If that sounds appealing, I invite you to continue. You are magic and so worth it.

PART 1

MULADHARA (ROOT)

The root chakra (Muladhara) is the first of the seven major chakras.

PRONOUNCED: *moo-laa-DHAA-ruh. Meaning: mūla = root; ādhāra = support, hold, base, foundation. The corresponding verbs are to* have *and to* be. *This chakra develops between ages one and seven.*

LOCATION

The base of the spine, in the tailbone area

ASSOCIATED COLOR

Red

KEY CONCEPTS

- Faith
- Family/tribe
- Grounding
- Home
- Physical identity

- Prosperity
- Safety
- Security
- Stability
- Trust

The root chakra's purpose is survival, security, and stability in your day-to-day life. Think about what makes you feel grounded, stable, safe, and secure. This chakra is linked to our basic needs for food, water, and shelter as well as to our emotional needs for connection, trusting what is happening around us, and being fearless. When these needs are met, we feel grounded and safe. This is the chakra of our foundation. Imagine a home, a strong concrete foundation rooted in the earth that provides a sturdy ground upon which to live life. The root chakra gives us the motivation to eat, sleep, and take care of ourselves. It is the foundation of our life force energy.

The root chakra is also associated with the physical body, including the adrenal glands, colon, kidneys, skeleton/bones, and muscles, as well as the arterial blood that flows through the left chamber of the heart, carrying oxygen and nutrients to our body tissue.

Root chakra energies give us a place for our lives to take root and for the flow of energies to propel us forward.

When root chakra energies are stuck, stagnant, imbalanced, or blocked, our vitality and zest for life are compromised. This can happen when our sense of belonging in the world is threatened or is experienced as traumatic, leaving us feeling a deep sense of insecurity.

Signs of a Balanced, Unblocked Muladhara Chakra

A balanced and open root chakra helps you feel grounded, secure, and at peace with the world and your world. You feel safe and able to take on life and its challenges with ease.

Signs of a Blocked Muladhara Chakra

Insecurity, restlessness, and anger indicate a blocked root chakra. You may feel stuck and inactive and experience overwhelming stress. You could experience change in your financial situation, struggles with relationships, stress in your day-to-day activities, or fight-or-flight responses.

Signs of an Overactive Muladhara Chakra

An overactive root chakra will cause feelings of anxiety, panic, and fear, as your basic need to survive may feel threatened. You may feel the energy of paranoia, nervousness, aggression, overeating, or stress eating.

I am connected with my higher, glowing self, always supported by the universe. I am connected to the earth, grounded in safe, deep-rooted love.

ROOT CHAKRA CHECKLIST/SELF-DIAGNOSIS

Use this checklist to determine if your root chakra is out of balance. If you check three or more boxes, you could benefit from giving your root chakra some attention.

BLOCKED/UNDERACTIVE/OVERACTIVE SYMPTOMS

- ☐ Craving sweet, salty, high-fat comfort foods
- ☐ Exercising significantly more or less than normal
- ☐ Feeling confused about your future and purpose
- ☐ Feeling disconnected from the world

- ☐ Feeling unusually depressed
- ☐ Fixating on material possessions
- ☐ Having frequent feelings of anxiety
- ☐ Having frequent feelings of fatigue
- ☐ Having trouble determining boundaries

- ☐ Neglecting your personal care
- ☐ Questioning life, love, and/or career
- ☐ Staying home due to sadness or anxiety

How do you feel safe in your life?

How do you feel unsafe in your life?

....
....
....
....
....
....
....
....
....
....
....
....
....
....
....
....

Where in your life do you need to show more appreciation (gratitude) for what is in front of you?

....

....

....

....

....

....

....

....

....

....

....

....

....

....

....

....

....

Where in your life can you set more boundaries?

How would being safe, setting boundaries, and being appreciative make you feel?

....

....

....

....

....

....

....

....

....

....

....

....

....

....

....

....

....

What grounds your energy and helps you feel less anxious?

NUTRITION FOR THE ROOT CHAKRA

List foods that nourish your root chakra. Some examples include beets, cayenne pepper, kidney beans, mushrooms, raspberries, red potatoes, and rosemary. Get creative; create your own meal or search online for recipes for root chakra nourishment. Then get cooking! Enjoy a healthy meal for the day or make enough for leftovers.

List all the places where you feel safest and most comfortable. Spend time in these safe and comfortable environments or bring their calming elements into your existing space. Add the color red—signifying the root—and/or earthy colors to remind you of nature. For example, place a mini fountain on your office desk or add art in your home that has colors of the earth.

ESSENTIAL OIL THERAPY FOR
THE ROOT CHAKRA

The root chakra corresponds with the sturdy earth element and feeling grounded, so when you want to heal this chakra with essential oils, turn to woodsy oils from trees that promote stability, such as cedarwood or sandalwood. Vetiver is another root-balancing oil. Diffuse the oils or apply them to your pulse points. In the space provided, write how you are feeling in the moment, releasing all that you are holding in onto the paper. Then allow yourself to really breathe in and connect to the essential oil scents, balancing your root.

MEDITATION AND SOUND

Chant "LAM," the associated sound for the root chakra. Close your eyes, take three deep inhales and exhales, and then chant "LAM" five times. Really extend the syllable, feeling the vibration within you opening your root chakra. Repeat as many times as needed.

CONNECT TO NATURE

Engage more in activities close to nature such as gardening, sunrise or sunset walks, walking with bare feet on the grass, or hiking.

CORRESPONDING CRYSTALS

Acquire some crystals that open the root chakra: black or green crystals such as black tourmaline, hematite, and onyx; or red stones such as red agate and red jasper. For just a few minutes a day, close your eyes, hold the crystal, and think about the intention of the red root chakra opening. Wear the crystal around your neck, place it in your pocket or under your pillow, or simply keep it close to you while working. Place your crystals as shown in the crystal grid on the following page for more crystal enhancement. Crystal grids help you direct, channel, and focus energy; even if you are not certain about the power of crystal healing, grids can be a beautiful reminder of your intentions.

PART 2

SWADHISTHANA (SACRUM)

The sacral chakra (Swadhisthana) is the second of the seven major chakras.

PRONOUNCED: *svaa-dhisht-HAA-nuh. Meaning: sva = the self; adhiṣṭhāna = location, basis, seat, place, "dwelling place of the self," supporting self-worth, personal expansion, and exploration of sexuality, desires, and creativity. The corresponding verb is to feel. This chakra develops between ages eight and fourteen.*

LOCATION ON THE BODY

Lower abdomen, about two inches below the navel

ASSOCIATED COLOR

Orange

KEY CONCEPTS

- Change (ability to flow through change)
- Connections
- Emotions
- Feelings
- Intimacy

- Joy of life
- Movement
- Passion
- Pleasure
- Sensation

The sacral chakra seeks pleasure, enjoyment, and connection to others. It is the powerhouse of emotional placement, motivation in life, day-to-day energy, creative expression, authentic creation, soul fire, and how we experience sexuality.

Some of its corresponding physical body areas and organs are the ovaries and genitals, lower back, abdomen, bladder, and kidneys. Its mental energy/feelings can link to depression and self-worth.

A balanced sacral chakra brings balance and harmony. Emotions flow without judgments, enhancing our ability to understand life deeply and to express and achieve our desires. We will be able to confidently and easily pull energy for creativity, movement, procreation, desire, pleasure, and deep connection in relationships. We freely express our wants and needs in relationships because we understand them.

Signs of a Balanced, Unblocked Swadhisthana Chakra

A balanced sacral chakra assists with healthy, easy creative expression; balanced hormones; and the ability and desire to experience pleasure. We find we are generous and giving because our energy is full, we are nurturing ourselves, and we create healthy boundaries without guilt. A balanced sacral chakra can take risks, be spontaneous with our soul's desires, and experience positivity and compassion.

Signs of a Blocked Swadhisthana Chakra

A sacral chakra can be mainly blocked by guilt and lack of creativity and spark for life. You may judge yourself negatively and feel inadequate and insufficient. You may have trouble engaging in pleasurable sexual relationships. You may hold negative, tired, and/or guilty ideas about physical intimacy and sex. You may feel disconnected from other people. You could feel you deserve punishment and may desperately search for worthy friends and/or partners, failing to realize that you are lovable.

Signs of an Overactive Swadhisthana Chakra

An overactive sacral chakra may cause an excessive sex drive, compulsive behaviors, extreme emotions, and emotional dependency on others.

I am a sacred being. I am worthy of love and desirable to others.

It is my birthright to receive pleasure and have my creative needs met.

SACRAL CHAKRA CHECKLIST/SELF-DIAGNOSIS

Use this checklist to determine if your sacral chakra is out of balance. If you check three or more boxes, you could benefit from giving your sacral chakra some attention.

BLOCKED/UNDERACTIVE/OVERACTIVE SYMPTOMS

☐ Comparing your-self to others

☐ Emotional depen-dency on others

☐ Excessive or non-existent sex drive

☐ Feeling insecure or having low self-esteem

☐ Feeling jealous

☐ Feeling lack of desire or passion

☐ Feeling out of touch with creativity

☐ Feeling tense or frustrated

☐ Feeling unemo-tional or unexcited

☐ Frequent mood swings

☐ Inability to focus

☐ Overindulging in toxic behaviors (drink-ing, smoking, eating unhealthy foods)

NUTRITION FOR THE SACRAL CHAKRA

List foods that nourish your sacral chakra. Some examples include cinnamon, dark chocolate, mangos, oranges, pumpkin seeds, raw honey, sweet potatoes, and turmeric. Get creative and build your own meal or search for recipes for the sacral chakra and then cook them up. Enjoy a healthy meal for the day or the week.

CONNECT WITH WATER

The sacral chakra is associated with the water element and symbolizes the power of flow. Connecting with water, such as a lake, a river, or the ocean, helps promote balance in the sacral chakra. If you can't get to a water element in nature, taking a long shower or warm bath to regulate emotions and empower and activate this chakra is great, too.

ESSENTIAL OIL THERAPY FOR THE SACRAL CHAKRA

Some great options for the sacral chakra are bergamot, jasmine, orange, patchouli, rose, sandalwood, sage, and ylang-ylang. Diffuse the oil or apply it to your pulse points. In the space provided, write how you are feeling blocked creatively, sexually, and/or emotionally in the moment, and release all that you are holding in onto the paper. Allow yourself to really connect to the essential oil scents you are diffusing and feel your sacral chakra opening.

MEDITATION

Meditation plays a vital role in balancing and opening all chakras, but we can make it specific. Chakra meditation helps us focus on the positive and discard negative thought patterns. Open YouTube or an app—my personal fave is the Insight Timer app—and search for "sacral chakra meditation" or "open sacral chakra." Find a short meditation to do in the morning, between work meetings, or right before bed (my favorite). A sleep-focused sacral chakra meditation will nourish us at the end of the day and even while we are sleeping.

COLOR THERAPY FOR THE SACRAL CHAKRA

Introduce subtle or bright shades of orange into your home, office, and wardrobe—clothes, artwork, jewelry, and even nails—to help heal and activate sacral energy flow.

YOGA

If you make yoga a part of your daily life, you are on your way to becoming more balanced in mind, body, and soul. Anyone at any age can benefit from these practices. Roll out your mat and practice yoga asanas (postures) that target the sacral area, such as happy baby, goddess, cow face, pigeon, and squat (Malasana). Search online for examples of the poses and for sacral chakra yoga flow practices.

PART 3

MANIPURA (SOLAR PLEXUS)

The solar plexus chakra (Manipura) is the third of the seven major chakras.

PRONOUNCED: *muh-ni-POOR-uh. Meaning: maṇi = a prized necklace of jewels or pearls, city of gems; pūra = to fill, full, fulfilling. The corresponding verbs are* can *and* to do. *This chakra develops between ages fifteen and twenty-one.*

LOCATION ON THE BODY

The upper abdomen, just below the rib cage

ASSOCIATED COLOR

Yellow

KEY CONCEPTS

- Development of the self
- Digestion
- Freedom from shame
- Metabolism
- Personal identity

- Powerful ambition
- Self-confidence
- Self-esteem
- Self-worth
- Warrior energy

The solar plexus chakra is associated with ambition, willpower, self-esteem, and the ability to rule as the god or goddess of your domain. Your power and self-confidence manifest in this chakra. It motivates you to strive toward success and good health and a deep understanding of who you are and why you are here.

Its corresponding physical body includes energy levels, weight gain and loss, digestive/gut health, and efficient absorption of nutrients.

The solar plexus chakra relates to feeling confident and in flow, with a strong handle on your life. Think of the last time you had butterflies or felt a pit in your stomach: That's the solar plexus at work. If the gut feels good, the excited energy is flowing; if it feels anxious, something is toxic or does not fit.

When the solar plexus—the body's energy powerhouse—is in balance, we feel free to express our true selves with confidence. If it is blocked, we may feel overwhelming amounts of shame and self-doubt, lacking the ability to take care of ourselves. We may also feel powerless, stagnant, or quick to anger.

Signs of a Balanced, Unblocked Swadhisthana Chakra

When the solar plexus chakra is balanced, you feel confident, responsible, spontaneous, playful, and reliable. You can make decisions and meet challenges with grace and ease. You feel an inner fire within, healthy energy levels, and high self-esteem.

Signs of a Blocked Swadhisthana Chakra

The solar plexus chakra is blocked mainly by shame and lack of self-worth. You may feel trapped, weak, powerless, vulnerable, and unable to share your vulnerability with others. Digestive issues are frequent. This chakra is associated with ambition and personal power, so blockages result in frustration, lack of direction, and anger. You may not be assertive enough to define your choices. You suffer from a lack of self-confidence and the courage to follow your dreams, and you seek external validation. You feel that you are a victim of circumstances.

Signs of an Overactive Swadhisthana Chakra

An overactive solar plexus chakra may cause you to feel overly aggressive, bossy, controlling, power hungry, competitive, attracted to sedatives, conceited, and self-centered. You could become overly rigid and need to be right. These qualities can feel harsh, but you must be honest with yourself if any of these energies are within you, directed toward yourself and/or others. Act by understanding these feelings, clearing them, and getting your chakra open, flowing, and balanced.

I am worthy.
I honor the power within me.

SOLAR PLEXUS CHAKRA
CHECKLIST/SELF-DIAGNOSIS

Use this checklist to determine if your solar plexus chakra is out of balance. If you check three or more boxes, you could benefit from giving your solar plexus chakra some attention.

☐ Being overly aggressive

☐ Experiencing blocked/ underactive/over- active symptoms

☐ Experiencing slow digestion/diges- tive issues

☐ Experiencing victim mentality

☐ Feeling attached to sedatives

☐ Feeling low in energy and slothful

☐ Feeling no trust in others

☐ Feeling the need to be right

☐ Feelings of low self-esteem

☐ Giving more of your- self than you have

☐ Having little or no willpower

☐ Lacking confi- dence in abilities

☐ Taking on too much responsibility

NUTRITION FOR THE SOLAR PLEXUS CHAKRA

List foods that nourish your solar plexus chakra. These include bananas, sunflower seeds, yellow peppers, eggs, salmon, pineapple, cumin, chamomile, and mint. Get excited to take care of *you*. Create your own or search for recipes for the solar plexus chakra—maybe a new dinner recipe or a fresh smoothie routine. Shop for the items and make a meal for the day or week—leftovers are great—that nourishes your solar plexus in a healthy way.

ESSENTIAL OIL THERAPY FOR
THE SOLAR PLEXUS

Use clary sage to promote relaxation and relieve depression juniper to clear blockages and improve digestion; and geranium to regulate hormones and detox the lymphatic system. Diffuse the oil or use on pulse points. In the space provided, write how you are feeling blocked in your self-worth and where you have a victim mentality or feel inadequate in the moment. Are you too controlling in certain areas of your life? Where can you let go? Just write and release all that you are holding in onto the paper. Then allow yourself to really connect to the essential oil scents you are diffusing. Feel your solar plexus chakra opening.

MIRROR-GAZING AND AFFIRMATIONS

Stand in front of the mirror, look yourself in the eye, and say the following words to yourself out loud over and over, getting louder each time:

I am enough.

I am worthy.

I am capable.

I am powerful.

Although it may feel uncomfortable, the louder you raise your voice, the more powerful this exercise becomes. Please don't let the discomfort stop you. Keep raising your voice and your high vibrations until you are screaming with confidence at yourself in the mirror.

MEDITATE AND DRAW

Close your eyes, imagine a glowing yellow light in your abdomen, and visualize the solar plexus yellow wheel, or circle. Visualize a sunflower grow within the chakra and begin to feel the opening and flow in a healthy, vibrant way. When you open your eyes, freely draw this beautiful yellow sunflower and flowing wheel as you visualized it.

CONNECT WITH YOUR INNER CRITIC

List all the ways you judge yourself. Include all the things you don't like about yourself and areas in which you tend to judge yourself harshly, such as physical traits, behaviors, or perceived weaknesses. Then close your eyes, take some deep inhales and exhales, and allow a visualization of yourself to come to life. Silently tell yourself that these characteristics are perfect as they are. Silently affirm and welcome all the qualities on your list. Say thank you to your inner critic for teaching you and protecting you all these years. Decide you are confidently moving forward without this judgment and low vibrational critic, and release it.

BRING ON THE CORE WORK

Big sigh, I know. Core—aka *solar plexus*—work is difficult but worth it, because every time you do it, you are burning through some of your self-limiting beliefs. So set aside ten minutes. Start with a forearm plank, feel your core muscles engage, and breathe. Inhale and exhale slowly and hold the pose longer than you think you can. (You may do this with your knees on the floor, if necessary.)

Before you begin the plank, set a timer for ninety seconds; when the timer goes off, stay in the pose. Every time you think it's impossible to keep going, keep going. Aim for a three-minute plank, but don't overdo it. Do what you can; you can continue or stop when you feel ready to stop. You can insert any core exercise you like that is physically accessible to you—crunches, leg raises, seated knee lifts, and so on. Keep track of your progress by recording the date and the duration of your solar plexus core work each time you do it.

PART 4

ANAHATA (HEART)

The heart chakra (Anahata) is the fourth of the seven major chakras.

PRONOUNCED: *uh-naa-HUH-tuh. Meaning: unstruck, true. The corresponding verb is to love. This chakra develops between ages twenty-two and twenty-eight.*

LOCATION ON THE BODY

At the heart center and extending through the arms and hands

ASSOCIATED COLOR

Green

KEY CONCEPTS

- Acceptance
- Balance
- Compassion
- Empathy
- Forgiveness
- Inner peace
- Joy
- Nurturing
- Relationships
- Unconditional love of self and others

The heart chakra is associated with—you guessed it—love, empathy, unity, healing, balance, relationships, and compassion. How you are in relationship to yourself, to others, and to the world is the major energy that sits in the heart chakra.

Some of its corresponding physical body connections are the thymus gland, lungs, shoulders, upper back, heart, and circulatory system.

Imagine that the heart chakra helps keep the channels of the heart open, allowing us to give and receive freely. An open heart chakra invites us to flow with ease on the different levels of relationship experiences in our lives. It assists not just romantic love, but love among family, friends, strangers, and all living things. It is believed that the stronger the heart chakra, the more love, compassion, and empathy a person can feel, experiencing more gratitude and joy. The heart chakra is also associated with peace, helping you gain harmony by loving and accepting yourself.

When the heart is open, a person feels optimistic, friendly, and motivated to believe in themselves. Building fulfilling relationships becomes easier when the heart chakra is balanced.

Energetically speaking, the heart chakra is the *center*—the bridge between the lower (root, sacral, solar plexus) and upper (throat, third eye, crown) chakras.

Signs of a Balanced, Unblocked Anahata Chakra

If the heart chakra is in balance, you will feel joy, gratitude, love, and compassion for those around you. You will feel deeply, believe that we are all interconnected, and show love to others and to yourself. You can let go of past experiences and forgive others easily, moving on rather than holding grudges. You can understand others' ideas, thoughts, and boundaries with acceptance and compassion. You find it easy to be empathetic and understand what others are going through.

Signs of a Blocked Anahata Chakra

Issues with heart chakra energy flow can make us feel lonely, isolated, and unable to love and connect to ourselves or others. When we are wounded and feel stuck in the past, it can lead to sadness and anxiety. You may feel afraid of sharing and trusting in some relationships. Any childhood disappointment can block this chakra, affecting your behavior as an adult. Any of these symptoms could indicate that the heart chakra needs to rebalance and heal: fear of rejection, loss of trust in a committed relationship, issues with giving and receiving affection, overdependency in a relationship, distant behavior with people who care, and tough and unemotional appearance while feeling vulnerable.

Signs of an Overactive Anahata Chakra

An overactive heart chakra can feel overly empathetic, overly concerned, overly sacrificing, jealous, unable to set boundaries for yourself, codependent, or clingy, with a tendency to stay in abusive relationships.

I am open to love.
I live in balance, in a state
of grace and gratefulness.

HEART CHAKRA CHECKLIST/SELF-DIAGNOSIS

Use this checklist to determine if your heart chakra is out of balance. If you check three or more boxes, you could benefit from giving your heart chakra some attention.

- ☐ Being dependent on others for happiness
- ☐ Being overly empathic
- ☐ Experiencing jealousy
- ☐ Falling in love frequently and quickly
- ☐ Feeling antisocial

- ☐ Feeling judgmental of others
- ☐ Feeling shy or timid
- ☐ Feeling unloved or unwanted
- ☐ Feelings of codependency
- ☐ Feelings of loneliness

- ☐ Tending to sacrifice self for others
- ☐ Testing others to prove their love

Finish the sentences "I feel shut down when . . .", "I reject myself when . . . ", "The first time I felt heartbreak was . . ." Allow yourself to write as many instances as come to mind. Keep writing on the topic until you feel you have written down as many experiences as you can.

Is there anyone you have not forgiven yet? Is there anyone you feel hurt you? First, write out all the hurt still inside your heart for those who come to mind. Spill out any details you have onto paper, in a physical release. Then take a deep breath and write, "Thank you [each person's name] for the gift of this pain, as I am growing deep happiness out of it." You may adjust this sentence to list any other gifts you may gain—strength, assuredness in yourself, rebirth, or confidence.

This chakra loves to bask in the energy of love. Write out a list of twenty things that make you feel loved.

List ten things you are grateful for that you do not consciously think of daily, such as clean water or healthy food. List ten other things you are grateful for that have not happened yet. Write them in past tense, as if they already happened.

How can you show yourself more self-love?

Do you find it easier to give or receive? Why?

....

....

....

....

....

....

....

....

....

....

....

....

....

....

....

....

....

NUTRITION FOR THE HEART CHAKRA

Foods that help open the heart chakra include avocado, broccoli, celery, chard, cucumber, dandelion greens, green apples, green tea, kale, lime, matcha, mint, parsley, peas, spinach, spirulina, and zucchini. So get creative. Get in the kitchen. Create your own recipe for breakfast, lunch, or dinner, and write it in the space provided.

ESSENTIAL OIL THERAPY FOR
THE HEART CHAKRA

Oils that open the heart chakra include eucalyptus, geranium, lime, marjoram, melaleuca, peppermint, rose, thyme, and ylang-ylang. Choose three that you will dedicate as your go-to scents for opening the heart chakra.

CHANT "YAM" AND JOURNAL

The heart chakra is associated with love. If you are not feeling loved or are experiencing difficulties in your relationships, try this chanting and journal exercise. "YAM" is the associated sound vibration for the heart chakra. Take ten minutes, close your eyes, take three deep inhales and exhales, and then chant "YAM" five times. Really drag out the syllable and feel the vibration within you open your heart chakra. Repeat as many times as needed to feel an openness within. In the space provided, write how you are feeling about your current relationships with yourself and others. Where is change needed? What do you need more of? What do you need to release to be open to giving and receiving love? Just write and release all that you are holding in onto the paper.

GREEN NUTRITION

The predominant color of the heart chakra is green. To balance this chakra, eat a diet filled with green for seven days, plus drink at least eight cups of water a day. Eating foods the same color as the chakra you are trying to heal and nourish can balance the energy flow around that area; in this case, they include green apples, green tea, and matcha along with broccoli, cucumbers, kale, and other green vegetables. Document your daily water intake and what green foods you ate and how much. Add a few sentences about how your heart energy feels each day.

MEDITATE AND DRAW

Visualize a lotus flower or a green hexagon, formed by two interlacing triangles, with a tiny bright flame burning at the center. Imagine it to be steady in a windless place. Allow this flame to burn brightly in your heart. Open your eyes, and draw what this lotus flower or hexagon looked like.

PRANAYAMA, BREATHING EXERCISES FOR THE HEART CHAKRA

The heart chakra element is air, so breathwork is a gateway to opening it. Anulom vilom, a core yoga breathing exercise also known as *alternate nostril breathing*, is one of the most beneficial breathwork techniques to balance the left and right hemispheres of the brain and open the heart.

Practicing anulom vilom frequently brings calmness to both body and mind through conscious breath regulation. When you breathe with more awareness, you allow your body to become fully oxygenated.

Inhale through one nostril while keeping the other closed with the thumb; then close the other side with the index finger. Retain the breath for a short while; then exhale out through the other nostril. Repeat this process with the other nostril. Set a timer and repeat for two minutes.

PART 5

VISHUDDHA (THROAT)

The throat (Vishuddha) chakra is the fifth of the seven major chakras.

PRONOUNCED: *VISH-uud-huh. Meaning: vi = apart; śuddhi = purification. The corresponding verb is to speak. This chakra develops between ages twenty-nine and thirty-five.*

LOCATION ON THE BODY

Center of neck/throat

ASSOCIATED COLOR

Blue

KEY CONCEPTS

- Assertiveness
- Clarity of speech
- Communication
- Creative expression
- Expressing truth and being receptive to others
- Expression of your will
- Listening
- Openness
- Self-expression

The throat chakra is associated with expression and communication, not only between the self and others but also between our own minds and bodies. The throat chakra connects our ability to speak, listen, sing, express our thoughts creatively, and let our true selves show.

Some corresponding physical body connections are the thyroid gland, vocal cords, mouth, tongue, jaw, shoulders, ears, and teeth. Situated between the third eye chakra (seat of intuition) and the heart chakra (seat of our emotions), the throat chakra bridges emotions and intellect.

The throat chakra voices our intuition and the heart chakra, and it controls our ability to communicate our personal power. When it's functioning at full capacity, this chakra allows us to express ourselves truly and clearly. Someone with a blocked throat chakra will feel like they have trouble finding the words to say how they truly feel. The inner self-talk will be harsh and depressing.

Someone with an open throat chakra will enjoy exploring themselves and the different viewpoints around them. They strive to create understanding and can keep their minds open. They express freely and calmly communicate during disagreements.

Signs of a Balanced, Unblocked Vishuddha Chakra

When this chakra is open, you may feel it is easy to be a good listener, you communicate easily and clearly, you live life creatively with expression of the heart and love, you speak with confidence, and you sing well even if you don't "sing well," expressing your soul through song. You express yourself freely without lies or guilt, you are comfortable with body language, and it feels easy to offer people sound advice.

Signs of a Blocked Vishuddha Chakra

When the throat chakra is blocked, you may neglect self-care and experience an inability to communicate and open up. You are scared of speaking the truth for fear of rejection. You always try to please everyone and struggle to speak up for your choices and ideas. You often feel unheard and misunderstood. You have a harsh inner voice.

Signs of an Overactive Vishuddha Chakra

When the throat chakra is overactive, you may talk to excess, cut others off, stutter, struggle to listen, gossip, speak in a loud or dominating voice, interrupt, and/or be overopinionated, critical, and bossy.

I speak my truth freely and openly.

My expression of my authentic truths attracts what I deserve.

How in your life are you speaking your truth—what you know or believe to be true? How in your life are you not speaking your truth?

....

....

....

....

....

....

....

....

....

....

....

....

....

....

....

....

Are you holding in any feelings? How would speaking your truth and expressing yourself fully make you feel?

....

....

....

....

....

....

....

....

....

....

....

....

....

....

....

....

How do you communicate in conflict?

When do you hesitate to use your voice?

Where do you want to be more authentic in your life?

When do you feel most creative, open, and free?

....

....

....

....

....

....

....

....

....

....

....

....

....

....

....

THROAT CHAKRA CHECKLIST/SELF-DIAGNOSIS

Use this checklist to determine if your throat chakra is out of balance. If you check three or more boxes, you could benefit from giving your throat chakra some attention.

☐ Are unable to focus

☐ Are unable to remember dreams

☐ Are overly critical

☐ Experience writer's block often

☐ Fear express-ing yourself

☐ Gossip frequently

☐ Have a shy or weak voice

☐ Have too many thoughts

☐ Suppress feelings

☐ Talk over others

☐ Talk too much

☐ Use hands exces-sively while talking

A HEALING VISUALIZATION AND DOODLE

Sit down in a quiet space and slowly observe your breath while taking deep, conscious inhales and exhales. Notice how your body feels and visualize your deep breathing as a cooling blue ball of light. Next, imagine this ball clearing space, pushing stuck energy out for you to speak and be heard. Don't worry if you lose your focus; just keep trying to come back to this cooling blue ball of light. Try to practice for five minutes at a time; after regular practice, your focus will improve. After you visualize, draw/doodle any images, words, or colors that you saw. Allow yourself to flow on the paper with creativity and an open throat chakra.

CHANT "HAM" AND JOURNAL

The throat chakra is associated with your physical, spiritual, mental, internal, and external voice. "HAM" is the associated sound vibration for the throat chakra. If you are not feeling able to openly communicate or your internal self-talk is very loud, try this chanting and journal exercise. Carve out ten minutes, close your eyes, take three deep inhales and exhales, and then chant "HAM" five times, drawing out the syllable. Feel the vibration from within you open your throat chakra. Repeat as many times as you need to feel an openness within. In the space provided, write how you are feeling about your inner voice. Has it been kind? How can you become nicer to yourself? Is there anything you want to say to someone? Are you holding truths within you or speaking to them? Just write and release all that you are holding in onto the paper.

CREATE YOUR OWN THROAT CHAKRA AFFIRMATIONS WITH A MEDITATION

Affirmations teach us to use the power of words with intention, clarity, and love. This can stimulate the throat chakra, which is our center for clear and intentional communication. Open a meditation app or YouTube and search for a short throat chakra meditation. Allow your mind to flow as it needs to as you drop deeper into the meditation. Be patient with yourself. While listening to the meditation, allow any words of empowerment to come to the surface. Once ready, write them in the space provided and create your own affirmations that resonate with your most authentic self. Repeat each affirmation by writing and speaking it five times. Anytime your throat chakra feels stuck or blocked, you can return to these affirmations.

NUTRITION FOR THE THROAT

To heal your throat chakra, turn to nutrition, too. Treat yourself with beverages such as coconut water or herbal teas and fruits that grow on trees, such as apples, pears, and plums. Research foods that nourish the throat chakra; make as long a list as you can.

CONSCIOUS MOVEMENT

Empower your throat chakra with meditative, conscious movement and release all the stuck energy in the blocked area. Adding simple movement will help you bring even more awareness into these areas and jump-start the flow of new energy.

Neck Stretches and Head Rolls

1. Sit in a cross-legged position or kneel.

2. Lift your right arm, reach over your head, and place your hand over your left ear.

3. Gently press your head toward your right shoulder. Draw your opposite arm toward the floor. Hold for a couple of breaths, and then repeat on the opposite side.

4. Next, interlace your fingers behind your head and pull your elbows back. Let your head fall back into your hands and hold for a few breaths. As you exhale, allow your head to drop forward. Hold here for a few deeper conscious breaths. Imagine the opening and flow of communication energy in your throat chakra.

5. Make head circles. Drop the head down; as you deeply inhale, roll your head to the right, and exhale as you roll to the left, landing back with the head/chin at beginning point.

6. Switch directions and repeat as many times as needed.

One of the best ways to open the flow of your throat chakra is through breathing exercises. Ujjayi breathing is a powerful form of yogic breathing.

Practice Ujjayi Breathing

1. Gently flutter your eyes shut.

2. Keep your lips sealed and focus on breathing in and out through your nose.

3. Inhale deeply through your nose and then exhale while constricting your throat muscles. Your breathing should resemble the sound of crashing waves—or Darth Vader.

4. Keep your lips sealed the whole time, breathing in through the nose and exhaling with lips sealed, building the energy within.

CREATIVE PROMPT

Journal or draw the sensations that come to mind after a period of ujjayi breathing. What did you see while you were practicing? How did your physical and mental energy shift as you breathed?

PART 6

AJNA (THIRD EYE)

The third eye (Ajna) chakra is the sixth of the seven major chakras.

PRONOUNCED: *AAJ-nyaa. Meaning: command, perceive, beyond wisdom. The corresponding verb is to see. It develops between the ages of thirty-six and forty-two.*

LOCATION ON THE BODY

Forehead between the eyebrows

ASSOCIATED COLOR

Indigo (dark blue/purple)

KEY CONCEPTS

- Ability to think and make decisions
- Deep understanding
- Discernment
- Good memory/dream recall
- Imagination
- Intuition

- Optimism
- Psychic abilities such as higher-level perception
- Visualization
- Watchfulness/awareness
- Wisdom

Our third eye chakra is our source of intuition, vision, imagination, and clairvoyance. This chakra represents our ability to see beyond our material selves. It is the chakra of insight, awareness, and light, linking to intuition and the ability to tap into logic and reasoning. A blockage can hamper your decision-making, especially as it relates to your dreams and goals.

A corresponding body connection is the pituitary gland, which regulates the endocrine system and hormone production. A third eye imbalance commonly causes headaches, hormone imbalances, nightmares, indecision, burnout, and lack of purpose.

The spiritual awareness resulting from the development of this sixth chakra can be overwhelming for those who have not built a healthy foundation in the lower five chakras. Once we have worked our way through those, the third eye begins to open. An inner knowing begins to rise, and we can clearly see ourselves. We see that "I am" is a moving target guided by intuition and deep trust. We are not our fears, our emotions, our beliefs, or our judgments. An open third eye sees life as the stage it is.

Signs of a Balanced, Unblocked Ajna Chakra

When the third eye chakra is in balance, you are more mindful, aware, and alert. Wisdom dawns on you easily, revelations arrive, and you tend to see everything from a broader and higher perspective with acceptance and clarity. You are more self-reflective and spiritually contemplative. You can think and see clearly without overthinking. When your third eye chakra works well, you feel full of alertness, clarity, and intuition. You just know what to do; answers, solutions, ideas, and insights come to you naturally.

Signs of a Blocked Ajna Chakra

When your third eye chakra is blocked, you are indecisive and can't make decisions, even after weighing the pros and cons. You may fail to trust your instincts, second-guessing a lot. You overthink about all things, large or small. You cannot hear and/or do not pay attention to your inner voice, reflections, and feelings.

Signs of an Overactive Ajna Chakra

When the third eye chakra is overactive, you may feel obsessed with your intuitive thoughts/ psychic visions, be paranoid, or have difficulty concentrating and a tendency to space out. Nightmares may happen more often.

I trust my intuition. I know the way.

I am connected to my soul purpose and my true path.

If you picture your most satisfied self, what does it look like?

When have you felt yourself listen to your intuition?

Where in your life may you be afraid to see the truth?

....

....

....

....

....

....

....

....

....

....

....

....

....

....

....

....

Do you feel balanced between optimism and reality?

....

....

....

....

....

....

....

....

....

....

....

....

....

....

....

....

....

Do you trust your own intuition and trust yourself to make good decisions? Do you make decisions based on what's logical or what feels right? Is there a healthy balance between the two?

....

....

....

....

....

....

....

....

....

....

....

....

....

....

....

....

If you could take a single step this week that leads you closer to your dreams, what would that look like? What does your intuition tell you? Can you take that step?

IDENTITY JOURNAL PRACTICE

Consider yourself as you are today (current self). Write down as many things you can think of that feel true right now that begin with "I am . . ." —for example, "I am a writer, I am a sister, I am a wife, I am happy, I am beautiful, I am lonely."

Next, imagine yourself ten years ago (past self), and create a similar list for yourself at that time. Finally, imagine yourself ten years from now (future self), and do the same thing.

Notice the differences in these lists. Reflect on how your sense of self has changed and how it wants to manifest.

ESSENTIAL OIL THERAPY FOR
THE THIRD EYE CHAKRA

Create your own third eye chakra scent. Purchase a handful of third eye chakra essential oils, such as bay laurel, clary sage, cypress, eucalyptus, frankincense, grapefruit, juniper, lavender, neroli, pure angelica, rose, sandalwood, sweet marjoram, and tea tree. Combine your choices to create a personal scent. In the space provided, record how many drops of each oil you use. My personal favorite third eye blend is three drops of frankincense, two of grapefruit, and one of lavender. Use your blend on your pulse points or diffuse to enhance third eye opening.

THIRD EYE CHAKRA CHECKLIST/
SELF-DIAGNOSIS

Use this checklist to determine if your third eye chakra is out of balance. If you check three or more boxes, you could benefit from giving your third eye chakra some attention.

- ☐ Being unable to distinguish imagination and reality

- ☐ Being unable to do mundane tasks

- ☐ Being unable to trust intuition, second-guessing a lot

- ☐ Being unaware of signs and synchronicities/ psychic sensations

- ☐ Feeling like you have a bad memory

- ☐ Feeling narrow-minded

- ☐ Feeling overly paranoid

- ☐ Frequently disassociating/spacing out

- ☐ Having a hard time remembering dreams

- ☐ Having trouble setting goals, daily and long term

- ☐ Overthinking/ experiencing a preoccupied, busy mind

- ☐ Struggling to function in daily life

FLAME MEDITATION AND DRAW/DOODLE

Ignite your third eye with this practice. Find a quiet space, play meditative sounds through an app such as Insight Timer or a sound machine with nature sounds, and light a favorite candle. Say this intention: "With this flame, I ignite and trust what my intuition is telling me. I am open to receive guidance."

Stare at the flame for three deep inhales and exhales; then close your eyes and imagine the flame in your third eye, between your eyebrows. Allow your third eye to imagine for a few minutes; then, in the space provided, doodle what you saw. Write down any intuitive guidance you received during this practice, acknowledging if you did not receive any. Consistently practicing this will help strengthen your third eye and intuitive voice.

KEEP A DREAM JOURNAL

The third eye is an active part of your ability to connect to your dreams while sleeping. The more you remember your dreams, the more connected you become to the unconscious and subconscious. Spend five to ten minutes every morning writing down everything you remember about your dreams. It helps to keep a pen and a writing pad or blank journal next to your bed so that you remember to write down your dreams each morning. If you cannot remember anything at all, spend this time in meditation, clearing your mind before turning on any electronic devices or getting active. You will eventually remember your dreams, because you are strengthening your third eye with meditation!

CHANT AND MEDITATE

Chant "OM" (or "AUM") to open this chakra. It will help open your awareness and intuitive guidance. Sit in a comfortable position in a chair or on the floor. Keep your spine erect, shoulders relaxed, and hands on the knees. Your jaw, stomach, and face should be totally relaxed and open to positive energy. Start by lightly bringing your index finger to the thumb, and gently close your eyes. Next, breathe slowly, inhaling and exhaling through the nose. With your eyes still closed, chant "OM," feeling the vibration within, and channel the vibrations to open your third eye. Practice this for at least five minutes.

PART 7

SAHASRARA (CROWN)

The crown (Sahasrara) chakra is the seventh of the seven major chakras.

PRONOUNCED: *suh-hus-RAA-ruh. Meaning: "thousand" or "infinite."*
The corresponding verbs are to know *and* to understand. *This*
chakra develops between the ages of forty-three and forty-nine.

LOCATION ON THE BODY

Top of the head

ASSOCIATED COLOR

Violet (white is often associated with this chakra as well)

KEY CONCEPTS

- Ability to surrender to a power higher than ourselves
- Brain function (memory)
- Connection to our higher selves
- Connection to the Divine, higher realms
- Our belief system
- Peaceful
- Revelation
- Sense of inner wisdom and trust
- Spiritual awakening and enlightenment
- Spirituality
- Transcendence

The crown chakra is the energetic connection to higher consciousness for greater understanding of this life—*your* life—assisting your universal identity and spirituality on this planet. Deep stuff, huh? The crown chakra provides the spiritual awareness that we are connected to something bigger than ourselves. It is deep trust for all that unfolds on our journey. Imagine this chakra is shaped like a tunnel, with its energy spiraling upward toward the spiritual realm.

Some corresponding physical body connections are with brain functions such as memory, intelligence, and sharp focus; the nervous system; the hypothalamus; and the pineal gland, which produces melatonin, the serotonin-derived hormone that affects our sleep-wake cycles.

When the crown chakra is in balance, we will feel connected to a source of higher power—the universe, God, universal love—and will feel we are living a higher purpose with full trust. This chakra relates to being at peace and embracing the human experience.

You will feel in balance among the body, mind, and spirit and able to live in a meditative state while keeping your mind open. Last, this chakra will help you feel connected to the higher realm and spirit guides or angels—those signs you see from above that become more magical with deeper connection and awareness.

Signs of a Balanced, Unblocked Sahasrara Chakra

When your crown chakra is balanced and open, you experience spiritual growth, infinite wisdom, and higher consciousness. By strengthening your connection to your spirit, or soul, you gain a sense of unity, power, and self-knowledge.

Signs of a Blocked Sahasrara Chakra

When your crown chakra is blocked, you often suffer from migraines and tension headaches. You may find you are more focused on tangible, materialistic possessions and disconnected from the spiritual realm. You often will feel loneliness, worthlessness, and meaninglessness. You avoid seeing any guidance from higher powers. You do not make it a priority to connect to your inner wisdom and happiness.

Signs of an Overactive Sahasrara Chakra

If your crown chakra is overactive, you may experience signs and symptoms of depression, insomnia, confusion, mental fogginess, lack of empathy, superiority, cynicism/skepticism, spiritual addiction (obsessing over signs you see or believing solely in one spiritual concept), self-destructive tendencies, and being overwhelmed by knowledge.

I honor the sacred divinity that exists within me. I am pure, beautiful, radiant light.

What does it mean to you to surrender? How do you practice surrendering? In what circumstances can you surrender more?

....

....

....

....

....

....

....

....

....

....

....

....

....

....

....

....

How do you honor your intuition?

....

....

....

....

....

....

....

....

....

....

....

....

....

....

....

Do you feel supported by a higher power?

....

....

....

....

....

....

....

....

....

....

....

....

....

....

....

In what ways do you try to control life?

How can you become more open-minded to different ways of thinking or being?

What is your sense of spirituality? How do you define it? How can you grow and learn more?

Imagine a day in which you are your highest and most authentic self, with a balanced crown chakra. How do you feel when you wake up? How do you move about your day? How do you speak to yourself and others? What self-care activities do you prioritize? Write about this day in the present tense, and as you write, allow yourself to feel the positive emotions you imagine yourself feeling.

GOOD MORNINGS

Check ten affirmations you will write and say out loud for five days straight, every morning after waking. Document how it makes you feel in the moment and how the rest of the day flows when you do this.

- ☐ I honor the sacred divinity that exists within me.

- ☐ I am pure, beautiful, radiant light.

- ☐ I am divinely protected, inspired, and guided by the universe.

- ☐ I surrender to the loving will of the universe.

- ☐ I am aligned with my purpose and truth.

- ☐ I am always divinely and lovingly guided.

- ☐ I release the need to control my life and surrender to a higher power.

- ☐ I trust my intuition and listen to the wisdom of the universe.

- ☐ I am always gently held and lovingly guided by this universe.

- ☐ I release doubt and welcome faith.

- ☐ Every day, I feel more connected to my spirit.

- ☐ I openly accept spiritual guidance from a higher power.

- ☐ I am love. I am light. I am connected to all.

COLOR THERAPY

Color therapy is surrounding yourself with the color of the chakra you intend to heal or activate. For the crown chakra, that means immersing yourself in all things violet (with a touch of white, if you'd like). Grab violet markers, crayons, and pencils, and doodle, drawing whatever comes to mind. As you draw, imagine your crown chakra opening, and let this act bring you peace and serenity. Imagine what feels like peace and serenity to you, and draw that.

SLEEP MEDITATION TO HEAL SUBCONSCIOUSLY

Open YouTube or Google and search "crown chakra sleep healing." Put some earbuds in to listen or play the recording next to your bed. Fall asleep to this meditation every night for five nights. Imagine your crown chakra as you listen and slip into sleep.

CROWN CHAKRA CHECKLIST/SELF-DIAGNOSIS

Use this checklist to determine if your crown chakra is out of balance. If you check three or more boxes, you could benefit from giving your crown chakra some attention.

- ☐ Feeling a sense of separation from life and oneself
- ☐ Having trouble trusting the universe
- ☐ Lacking belief in a higher power
- ☐ Lacking knowledge of purpose

- ☐ Feeling confused or lost
- ☐ Experiencing forgetfulness often
- ☐ Feeling addicted to spirituality
- ☐ Feeling disassociation from your body

- ☐ Criticizing/judging others' spirituality
- ☐ Feeling overwhelmed by knowledge
- ☐ Feeling confused or overloaded
- ☐ Struggling to define your individual identity

FIND THE FEELING OF AWE

Spending time in nature is the most potent way to experience awe. Set aside time on your calendar to get to the woods, mountains, or ocean. Look around you and feel the humility of how small we really are. Stargaze under the vast night sky or try to catch as many sunrises and sunsets as you can (sunsets are my personal favorite). Let nature move you with its majesty and magic. Bring this journal with you and jot down your thoughts as you take in the beauty all around you.

CORD PULLING/CUTTING/RELEASING

A cord-cutting meditation is an energetic process where you cut and pull to dissolve energetic ties to others. You can have energetic cords with a partner or an ex-partner, a parent, a friend, or a co-worker. You never know how much of other people's energies you've internalized until you pull the cords off. Search for "cord cutting/pulling" in a meditation app or online and immerse yourself in this practice of freedom, openness, and new beginnings.

A FINAL NOTE

Well, here you are at the end, magical soul—and at the beginning of a more magical, high-vibe you. When your chakras are balanced and your flow of energy is aligned, those pesky negative feelings and thoughts, as well as physical ailments, will be less likely to manifest.

I hope that you are now on your way to becoming your own guru—mastering your chakras and the power they represent. This transformation will assist you in moments of uncertainty, anxiety, doubt, fear, or stress; when you are feeling overwhelmed; or when trauma arrives or resurfaces from deep within—the list can go on. The more you turn to this journal and decide to go within to nourish each chakra, the more you become the radiant, successful, love- and light-filled being you are destined to be. Stay in your power by working with your energy every single day. Sending love and light!

RESOURCES

AliaSobel.com

Reiki energy healing helps open all the chakras. You can learn it on your own, but know that if you want assistance from a mentor or energy expert, seeking out a Reiki practitioner is highly advised. Alia offers virtual and in-person sessions.

Insight Timer App

Use this free meditation app as you see fit and allow it to become a part of your daily habits.

YouTube

You can search for mediation, yoga movement, and breathwork on YouTube to guide you on your journey.

REFERENCES

Alcantara, Margarita. *Chakra Healing: A Beginner's Guide to Self-Healing Techniques that Balance the Chakras.* Berkeley, CA: Althea Press, 2017.

Brown, Kalee. "How the Chakra System Relates to Our Ages & Stages of Development." Global Heart. January 31, 2019. globalheart.nl/spiritualiteit /chakra-system-chakras-relates-to-our-age-stages-of-development.

Powers, Lisa. *Reiki: Level I, II and Master Manual.* CreateSpace Independent Publishing Platform, 2016.

ABOUT THE AUTHOR

 **Alia Sobel** is the founder of the Two Word Story Mantra & Rebel Soul lifestyle. She is many things because her own traumas have shown her that our souls thrive by continually learning, evolving, and growing from what life sends us. Originally from Chicago, she now lives in Philadelphia. She has been married for fourteen years and is a proud mama, the best-selling author of *Legacy Speaks* and the *Rebel Soul Journal*, a Holy Fire™ and Usui Reiki master healer, a soul intuitive, an energy healer, a yoga teacher, and a Rebel Soul coach. Her mission is to empower the collective to honor its R.E.B.E.L. (Radiant. Elated. Balanced. Empowered. Loved.) soul. She helps those who are ready to rebelliously fall in love with themselves and confidently know what they must do to feel R.E.B.E.L.

Alia ignites the light, keeping that Rebel Soul spark ablaze within you, manifesting the life you are so worthy of. She holds space for this energy work through an immersive one-on-one four or eight-week program, the Rebel Soul Rebirth + Reiki certification, as well as through the Rebel Soul Reiki School (offering Level 1, Level 2, and Master Reiki certifications), through single Reiki sessions (in person or virtual), through spiritual retreats all over the world, and through sharing on social media and in print.